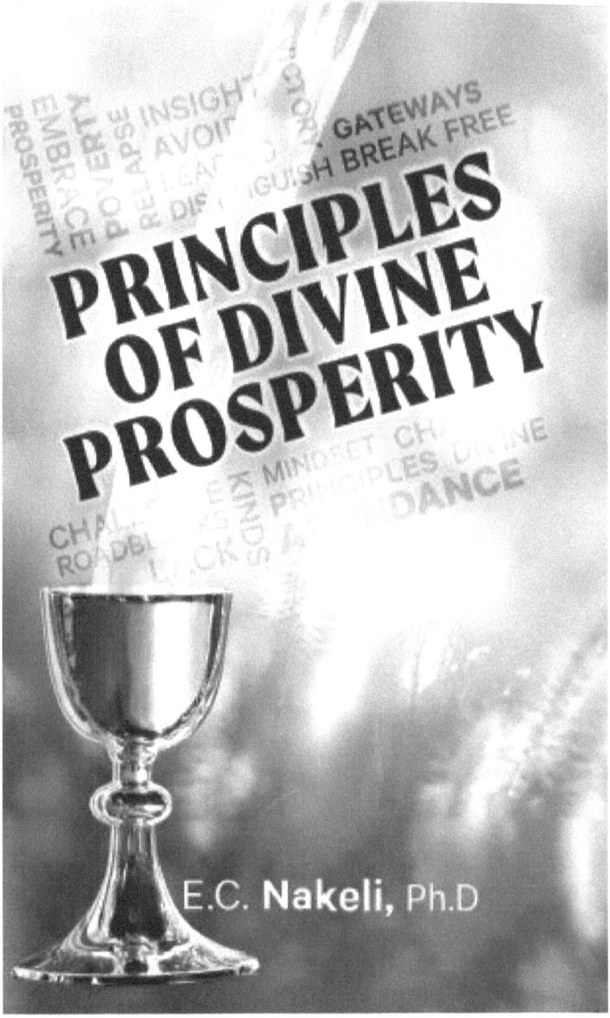

PRINCIPLES OF DIVINE PROSPERITY

E.C. **Nakeli**, Ph.D

Principles of Divine Prosperity

E.C. Nakeli, Ph.D.

© 2020 by E.C. Nakeli
Published by King's Word Publishing

For your questions and publishing needs, write to:
King's Word Publishing
40 S Church St
Westminster, MD 21157

Printed in the United States of America
All rights reserved. No part of this publication may be reproduced, stored in a retrieval systems, or transmitted in any form or by any means — for example, electronic, photocopy, recording — without the prior written permission of the publisher. The only exception is brief quotations in printed reviews.

To contact the author, write to:
E.C. Nakeli
Karlstrasse 4
75053 Gondelsheim
Germany
E-mail: *ecnakeli@yahoo.com*

Principles of Divine Prosperity/E.C. Nakeli
ISBN: 9781945055997
Unless otherwise indicated, Scriptures references are from
THE HOLY BIBLE, NEW INTERNATIONAL VERSION®, NIV®
Copyright © 1973, 1978, 1984, 2011 by Biblica, Inc™
Used by permission. All rights reserved worldwide.

Contents

Dedication viii

Acknowledgements ix

Preface x

Introduction 13
    The scope of divine prosperity 14
    Prosperity is God's will 15
    The basis for divine prosperity 16
    The engine of divine prosperity 17
    Two kinds of prosperity 18

Principle #1 20

The right mindset 20
    Poverty is a curse 20
    Poverty is an effect of laziness 23
    More than mere confession 23
    Pride 24
    Indiscipline 26
    Ancestral roots 27
    God transplanted Abraham 29
    Genealogy is important 30

Principle #2 36

Honesty and Integrity 36
    Honest business dealings 38

Pay your workers what they deserve 40

You can start all over 41

Slow and steady is better 42

Principle #3 44

Diligence 44

Two kinds of work 45

How to develop diligence 47

The rewards of diligence 53

Principle #4 55

Generosity 55

Be a money lender 56

The Secret 57

GOD WANTS YOU TO ABOUND 61

Principle #5 74

Faithfulness and consistency 74

Develop conviction 76

It takes discipline 77

When no one believes in you 79

Principle # 6 83

Surrendering 83

Not leaning on your understanding 85

Acknowledging the Lord in all your ways 86

Do not be wise in your own eyes 90

    People will seek your favor 91

    Friends in High Places.. 92

    To surrender is to submit.. 94

Principle #7.. 96

A strong relationship with Jesus 96

    The need for maturity 97

    What a strong relationship looks like 99

    The power of God's Word: 100

    Deciphering Divine instruction 101

    He sometimes speaks through others..................... 102

Principle #8.. 105

Understand the power of the blessing........................ 105

    The Power of the blessing 105

    Abraham Understood the power of the blessing... 107

    It worked for Jacob 108

    You are a candidate.. 109

Principle #9.. 111

Put God's Kingdom first... 111

    Working like an elephant, reaping like an ant...... 113

Principle #10.. 118

Sacrifice and Covenant with God................................ 118

    Covenant through sacrifice..................................... 118

    Covenant of Tithes and offerings 120

God´s challenge to you 121
In Conclusion 125

Dedication

I dedicate this book to my friend Apostle Robinson Fondong. You are a strong believer in divine prosperity and desire to see the saints of God enter into the fullness of prosperity God's way. May God use you to lead millions out of poverty, both mentality and physically, into divine prosperity.

Acknowledgements

Thank you to my beloved wife Madeleine , my most faithful partner in ministry. Thank you to my children Maaseiah, Mashal, and Loria. Thank you to my sister in-law Jeannette, a.k.a. Unlimited Greatness, my God-given translator into French. To all my partners in ministry, present and future. The Lord God richly bless you all.

Preface

Principles of Divine Prosperity is a book that was born as a result of a message I preached in the December 2019 International convention of EMEC Cameroon. I had been invited by my friend Apostle Bishop Robinson Fondong of Christian Missionary Fellowship International, Maryland USA to share the time that had been allotted him to minister during the convention. The day I was ministering, the International President of Christian Missionary Fellowship International and Associated Churches, Professor Bishop Joseph Mbafor, was also visiting the convention of several thousand individuals.

Two days after the ministry, he asked me for the copy of my book that contained the message I had preached. Unfortunately, I had custom prepared the message for the convention, and did not have a book on the theme. Other minsters who were present at the convention had also asked which of my books had the message. This demand is what led to the development of the message I had preached into this book you are now holding. Of course, the book contains details which couldn't be shared during the 45-minute-long message.

"Principles of Divine prosperity" is not a magic guide to becoming rich overnight. it is a book gleaned from years of experience and principles revealed in the Word as gateways to a prosperous life. It is my prayer and desire that as you read this book, beyond getting excited, you will actually invest time and implement these principles, so as to become prosperous God's way.

Introduction

"Beloved, I wish above all things that thou mayest prosper and be in health, even as thy soul prospereth" (3John1:2, KJV).

The word "prosper" used in this verse is from the Greek word "euodoō" which corresponds to Strong's number G2137, which means to passively succeed in reaching a goal, because you are helped on the road. It also means to have a prosperous journey, figuratively, to succeed in business affairs. Finally, it means to be led in a direct and easy way.

When the Bible talks about prosperity, it implies God Himself helping you to succeed in life's journey by making you take a direct and easy path where it would otherwise not be possible. The essence of divine prosperity is for things to increasingly get better. That is, if you look at your today, it should be better than yesterday, and your tomorrow should be better than today.

God has designed the path you take in life to be constantly improving. Proverbs 4:18 says, **"The path of the righteous is like the morning sun, shining ever brighter till the full light of day"**. That is, you move from brightness to brightness, from good to better, and from better to best. This is quite consistent with what the Bible teaches on other aspects.

For example, we are supposed to go from strength to strength (Psalm 84:7), from faith to faith (Romans 1:17), and from glory to glory (2Corinthians 3:18). It is true that one can meet momentary setbacks, but overall, when one looks at the big picture, things should look and get better with each passing day in life. There may be tunnels on our way, sometimes many of them, but there will always be light, brighter than before we met the tunnels.

The scope of divine prosperity

Divine prosperity is not centered around gold or silver, but it is about every facet of our lives. The phrase "above all things" can also be translated as "in everything" or "as concerns everything" or "in every regard". Therefore, a man who is wealthy, but has a broken home is not necessarily prosperous in Bible terms. A wealthy man with a bankrupt spiritual life is not prosperous by God´s standards. So, divine prosperity encompasses every aspect of our lives, social, spiritual, emotional, financial, professional, intellectual, mental etc.

Prosperity is God's will

When the apostle John wrote that he wished that the brethren prospered, he was not making a wishful thinking. The Greek word actually means to pray to God. He was therefore saying, "I pray to God that you prosper". This great apostle who had walked with God so many years by this time understood that it is God's will for His people to prosper.

It is written that **"The blessing of the Lord, it maketh rich, and he addeth no sorrow with it" (Proverbs 10:22, KJV).** Prosperity without sorrow is God's will for His people. It is also written that,

"**[17] You may say to yourself, "My power and the strength of my hands have produced this wealth for me." [18] But remember the Lord your God, for it is he who gives you the ability to produce wealth, and so confirms his covenant, which he swore to your ancestors, as it is today" (Deuteronomy 8:17-18).**

God gives you the ability to make wealth which is an aspect of prosperity. Hence prosperity cannot be wrong if it is the Lord who gives one the ability to prosper. This leads us to our next point.

The basis for divine prosperity

"For you know the grace of our Lord Jesus Christ, that though he was rich, yet for your sake he became poor, so that you through his poverty might become rich" (2Corinthians 8:9).

"[13] Christ redeemed us from the curse of the law by becoming a curse for us, for it is written: "Cursed is everyone who is hung on a pole."[14] He redeemed us in order that the blessing given to Abraham might come to the Gentiles through Christ Jesus, so that by faith we might receive the promise of the Spirit" (Galatians 3:13-14).

The basis for divine prosperity is the finished work of redemption on the cross of calvary. When Jesus died, He became sin that we might become holy. He became poor that we might become rich. He took our sicknesses that we might live in health. He was punished so that we might be free. Our redemption on the cross was from sin, sickness, poverty, and dominion by satan. It is incomplete and lopsided to emphasize one or more aspects of the redemptive work of the cross to the exclusion of others.

The engine of divine prosperity

The engine of divine prosperity is the soul. The soul is what determines how much a man or woman prospers in this life. The apostle John prayed that the church would prosper even as their soul prospers, that is, in the same way their soul prospers.

Divine prosperity is directly proportional to the prosperity of your soul. Remember that your soul consists of the mind, the will and the emotions. As we study the keys to divine prosperity, you will see how each aspect of our soul comes into play to determining the extent of our prosperity.

Two kinds of prosperity

You may have noticed that I have been laying emphasis on divine prosperity. This is because there are two types of prosperity. There is divine prosperity on the one hand, and the prosperity of the wicked (Psalm 73:3) on the other. Divine prosperity is in accordance with the principles, values, and ways of God as revealed in the Bible, while the prosperity of the wicked is that which violates the divine values, laws, and principles.

If I became rich and wealthy because I exploited and cheated others, my prosperity is the prosperity of the wicked and not divine prosperity. That is why there are men of God whose prosperity is the prosperity of the wicked and not divine prosperity, because they prey on the weak, the poor, the ignorant, and the vulnerable.

On the other hand, there are unbelievers whose prosperity is divine because it´s in line with biblical values. One thing you should understand about principles is that whoever applies them rightly benefits from them. It is possible to apply principles of financial prosperity and become rich while your soul is on its way to hell. This too, cannot be fully qualified as divine prosperity, because an important aspect of your life is not prospering, namely, the spirit. This leads us to the first key to divine prosperity: the right mindset.

Principle #1

The right mindset

The mind is the battleground of life. The state of your mind regarding the topic of divine prosperity is critical to entering your inheritance of divine prosperity. Let us look at critical areas in which your mindset must change:

Poverty is a curse

There are a lot of people who wrongly believe that poverty is a blessing. In other words, it is a reflection of spirituality. If you hold such a view, then you may remain poor all your life. Poverty is not and will never be a blessing. It is one thing to be rich and decide to live modestly because you are giving to the needs of others and to the work of the kingdom. It is something different when you cannot meet your own needs and have to depend on others to provide for you. Such a position makes your life miserable, because you are always prone to covetousness and jealousy. Look at what James says,

> **"What causes fights and quarrels among you? Don't they come from your desires that battle within you? ² You desire but do not have, so you kill. You covet but you cannot get what you want, so you quarrel and fight. You do not have because you do not ask God. ³ When you ask, you do not receive, because you ask with wrong motives, that you may spend what you get on your pleasures" (James 4:1-3).**

So, in a place where people´s desires cannot be met because they do not have the means, it is very likely that there would be fighting, quarreling, and even murder. It is easier for a poor man to be covetous and jealous of those who have. So, poverty exposes you to sin. That is why proverbs 10:15 says, **"The wealth of the rich is their fortified city, but poverty is the ruin of the poor" (Proverbs 10:15).**

Therefore, it is not the enemy of the poor who destroys them, it is not even the devil; the ruin of the poor is their poverty. Poverty is a destructive force, and no destruction is a blessing. In listing the curses of the law, Moses said,

"… therefore in hunger and thirst, in nakedness and dire poverty, you will serve the enemies the Lord sends against you. He will put an iron yoke on your neck until he has destroyed you" (Deuteronomy 28:48).

How can poverty be a blessing when it is listed as a curse? That would be a contradiction, wouldn´t it?

How on earth is it a blessing if you cannot eat to your satisfaction or drink healthy? How is it a blessing if you cannot dress well. How is it a blessing if you are sick or your child is sick and you cannot buy medication? I am laying emphasis on this because it is crucial for the deliverance of many.

If you believe poverty is a blessing, then God will not deliver you from a blessing, He only delivers from curses and harmful things. May God sow in your heart a holy hatred for poverty and all its manifestations, because they are signs one may be operating under a curse.

Poverty is an effect of laziness

There are people who are poor not because they are operating under a curse per se, but because they are lazy. Laziness is the root cause of the poverty of a great number of people. It is written that,

"Laziness brings on deep sleep, and the shiftless go hungry" (Proverbs 19:15) and

> **"A little sleep, a little slumber, a little folding of the hands to rest—[11] and poverty will come on you like a thief and scarcity like an armed man" (Proverbs 6:10-11).**

You see then, that laziness is an open door to the spirit of poverty. Poverty here referred to as an armed robber is a spirit that forces its way into a life through the door of laziness. So, while for some people a simple change in habits can break the chain of poverty, for others there is need to be administered deliverance from the spirit of poverty.

More than mere confession

While confessions and declarations are important, you cannot confess your way out of poverty. There is the need for calculated hard work.

We shall come to this later, but it suffices for us to emphasizes here that, **"Lazy hands make for poverty, but diligent hands bring wealth" (Proverbs 10:4)** and **"All hard work brings a profit, but mere talk leads only to poverty" (Proverbs 14:23).** Mere talk, whether you call them proclamations or declarations, by themselves, if not accompanied by corresponding action, they are a manifestation of laziness.

Pride

Another principal cause of poverty is pride. Pride has many manifestations, but here, I am concerned with two of its manifestations that lead to poverty. First, the inability to listen to advice or counsel and second, despise for little beginnings.

In regards to not being able to listen to, and obey wise counsel, the Bible says, **"Poverty and shame *will come* to him who disdains correction, but he who regards a rebuke will be honored" (Proverbs 13:18).**

Many people are in a cycle of rise and fall because they think they know it all. Others are stuck in the same place year after year because they think they know it all and would not listen to correction. There are people who have lost in a moment everything they worked so hard for because they failed to heed correction. How do you react to correction, especially from people with more of life´s experience?

In regards to despise for little beginnings, the Bible says, **"… Who dares despise the day of small things?" (Zechariahs 4:10).** In despising the day of small things, you forfeit the opportunity to grow. You fail to provide something which the Lord can bless and prosper as the work of your hands. What is it you can do? **"Though thy beginning was small, yet thy latter end should greatly increase" (Job 8:7)**. The beginning may seem small and unworthy, but applying the principles of prosperity will lead to increase and a glorious end.

Indiscipline

How does indiscipline lead to poverty? When you spend more than you earn, you are likely living in debt and, by living in debt you are working for your lenders, since you of course pay interest.

In God's will, those who are blessed are those who lend, and those who are cursed are those who borrow. Those who lend rule over those who borrow. As it is written, **"The rich ruleth over the poor, and the borrower is servant to the lender" (Proverbs 22:7).** Indiscipline is also manifested in all expenses and no investments.

> **"For the Lord thy God blesseth thee, as he promised thee: and thou shalt lend unto many nations, but thou shalt not borrow; and thou shalt reign over many nations, but they shall not reign over thee." (Deuteronomy 15:6)**
>
> **"The Lord will open the heavens, the storehouse of his bounty, to send rain on your land in season and to bless all the work of your hands. You will lend to many nations but will borrow from none" (Deuteronomy 28:12).**

You cannot reign over those you borrow from.

Ancestral roots

There are some people who are poor not because they are lazy, or proud or undisciplined. They work hard, are very disciplined with money, and listen to instructions, but when you look at their lives, there is nothing to show for all the hard work and discipline. Such people might be facing a limitation due to their ancestral heritage.

To illustrate, there are families made up of people who work extremely hard, however, no one has been able to break free from the grip of poverty. No matter how educated and enterprising they may be, poverty seems to be a stronghold. Sometimes, entire communities can be operating under this ancestral cause of poverty.

There are tribes of hundreds of thousands of people or even millions of people who are all operating under this ancestral curse or root of poverty. sometimes, it´s an entire nation that is bound by this ancestral root of poverty. You see vast natural, human, and intellectual resources yet there is nothing in the nation to show for it.

People who are operating under this ancestral root of poverty continue to manifest this poverty even after they come to Christ. This is not because our redemption does not include freedom from poverty, but because people are not taught that nothing in Christ is automatic. Whatever you fail to appropriate as your inheritance in Christ, you will not possess.

For example, Christ died for the sins of all mankind past, present, future yet some are still living in sin because they have not appropriated Christ as their salvation. Many who come to Christ are still plagued by one form of sickness until they have appropriated Christ as their healer and health. Unfortunately, very few are taught to deal with poverty in the same way.

The Lord Jesus became poor so that you may become rich. Although it is an accomplished fact, until you actively appropriate it by faith, it doesn't become a reality. To drive home the power one´s ancestral roots may have on you, let´s look at the case of Abraham.

God transplanted Abraham

In Genesis chapter twelve from verse one, God told Abraham

> **"Go from your country and your kindred and your father's house to the land that I will show you. ² And I will make of you a great nation, and I will bless you and make your name great, so that you will be a blessing. ³ I will bless those who bless you, and him who dishonors you I will curse, and in you all the families of the earth shall be blessed" (Genesis 12:1-3, ESV).**

Notice that Abraham's entering into the fullness of the blessing God was promising him was contingent on him being uprooted at several levels. Abraham needed to be separated from his national roots, his tribal roots, and his family roots. There had to be a threefold separation to fully enter the blessings God was promising him.

There is the principle that you must effectively separate in order to fully enter that which God has put before you. Remember that everything that was accomplished on the cross has to be appropriated and enforced by you. When God transplanted Abraham and blessed him, because he was separated at three levels, there was nothing that could hinder the blessings. Therefore, Abraham became the refence point in the genealogy of the Jewish people.

Genealogy is important

There is a principle of generational sins and the consequent curses that accompany them working in the lives of people several generations down the line. God is a God of generations. In Exodus 34:6-7, the Lord described Himself as,

> **"The Lord, the Lord, the compassionate and gracious God, slow to anger, abounding in love and faithfulness, [7] maintaining love to thousands, and forgiving wickedness, rebellion and sin. Yet he does not leave the guilty unpunished; he punishes the children**

and their children for the sin of the parents to the third and fourth generation" (Exodus34:6-7).

To properly deal with generational root system, you will need to go at least four generations back beginning with your parents, through grandparents on both sides, great grandparents on both sides, and great great grandparents of both sides. Carry out the necessary separations from the influence of their covenants, sins and everything negative that may have been passed on to you including the curse of poverty.

In Isaiah 51:1-2 the Lord told Israel,

> **"Hearken to me, ye that follow after righteousness, ye that seek the Lord: look unto the rock whence ye are hewn, and to the hole of the pit whence ye are digged.
> ² Look unto Abraham your father, and unto Sarah that bare you: for I called him alone, and blessed him, and increased him" (KJV).**

The Lord drew their attention to the fact that, their lives ought to be a reflection of their roots.

My questions to you are:

From what rock have you been cut?"

From what pit were you dug?

What do you see in the rock from which you were cut and in the pit from which you were dug? These are very important questions for you to consider.

I was ministering somewhere in Germany and asked how many people knew their father's name and every hand went up. I then asked those who knew their grandfather's name to keep their hands up, and some hands remained. When I asked how many people knew their great grandfather, only one hand remained. By the time I arrived the great great grandfather, there was no hand remaining. The majority of those present were people of African descent.

What your fore parents did may be affecting you today if you have not actively separated yourself from the links that attach you to their past. You did not fall from heaven. Although you have been born from above as a born-again believer, you have to appropriate it and establish it for yourself. And it begins by the threefold separation as recommended to Abraham by the Lord God Himself.

Who is the reference point in your genealogy?

In 1Samuel 9:1-2, when the Lord lists the genealogy of Saul, He goes back to the fifth generation. Normally the Bible usually goes back to the third or fourth generation, but in the case of Saul, the Bible goes back to the fifth generation, Aphiah. Aphiah was the reference point of Saul's genealogy because that word means to be rekindled or refreshed from the roots. There was a point in that family line where things were refreshed and rekindled after generations of turning away from God.

When you look back at your generations, is there a point where there was a refreshing? If not, you can become that point of refreshing by breaking free from the negative influences of the past generations. It is no doubt that the descendants of Aphiah were all wealthy and well to do men in Israel. Kish the father of Saul and Ner his brother were all wealthy men, and their children were the leaders of the Kingdom for over forty years.

If the poverty you are suffering from is due to generational influences, until you implement this threefold separation from your national, tribal, and family roots, nothing might be able to help you.

Understand your new root system

Many times, because of my African accent people ask me where I came from, and I often answer by saying I am a heavenian. When they ask what that means, I respond by saying it means I am from heaven. Sometimes I may go ahead and further tell them that I was originally from Cameroon, but now I come from heaven. You see, because I have been transplanted by God into His kingdom and have separated myself from the influences of my natural country of origin, I don´t automatically refer to it.

Your new nationality is heavenian, you have to actively declare your heavenly citizenship.

"But our citizenship is in heaven. And we eagerly await a Savior from there, the Lord Jesus Christ" (Philippians 3:20).

Not only do you have a new nationality, but you have a new tribe. Your tribe is Christian.

> **"But you are a chosen people, a royal priesthood, a holy nation, God's special possession, that you may declare the praises of him who called you out of darkness into his wonderful light" (1Peter 2:9).**
>
> **"Consequently, you are no longer foreigners and strangers, but fellow citizens with God's people and also members of his household" (Ephesians 2:19).**

And finally, your family is of Christ. You have been born from above into God's family.

> **"There is neither Jew nor Gentile, neither slave nor free, nor is there male and female, for you are all one in Christ Jesus. [29] If you belong to Christ, then you are Abraham's seed, and heirs according to the promise" (Galatians 3:28-29).**

Stop saying "that is how it is done in my country or tribe or family" you no longer belong there.

Principle #2

Honesty and Integrity

God had promised Abraham that He would bless him and make his name great among the nations. A few years later, in a sense, we can say Abraham had compromised by giving his wife out to Pharaoh, and in turn received a lot of goods and riches. The Lord then appeared to Abraham and told him,

> **"I am God Almighty; walk before me faithfully and be blameless. Then I will make my covenant between me and you and will greatly increase your numbers" (Genesis 17:1-2).**

God's covenant of increase and blessing was contingent upon Abraham walking blamelessly and faithfully. The fulfilment of the covenant of blessing was a consequence of his response to the Lord's admonishment.

I have seen believers; even professing men of God use underhanded means to gain advantage of others due to the quest to become rich and appear blessed. You do not need the methods of hell to enter into heaven's blessing. Blamelessness in enterprise is a sure path to true and lasting prosperity. That is why the writer of proverbs admonishes that, **"He that hasteth to be rich hath an evil eye, and considereth not that poverty shall come upon him" (Proverbs 28.22, KJV).**

When your goal is to become rich, you will develop an evil eye. An evil eye looks at others with the intent to take advantage of their vulnerabilities. It looks at systems for loopholes to exploit. It will not mind trampling on others, if only it leads to gain.

Look around and you see the society is littered with people who were once wealthy, but have nothing to show for today. In most of these cases, they hastened to become rich and used all means possible. They did not know that poverty was waiting to strike in the middle of the road.

Honest business dealings

Dishonest dealings should not be part of the transactions of God's people. Yes, God has used circumstances, time and again, to expose the fraudulent activities of some who name His Name. When the Lord chose a people for Himself and brought them out of Egypt, He asked them to be honest in their business dealings with one another and with the stranger. Deuteronomy 25:13-16 says,

> **"Do not have two differing weights in your bag-one heavy, one light. Do not have two differing measures in your house-one large, one small. You must have accurate and honest weights and measures, so that you may live long in the land the LORD your God is giving you. For the LORD your God detests anyone who does these things, anyone who deals dishonestly."**

As a Christian man or woman, decide that you will avoid dishonest business dealings. Do not appear to use accurate scales when you know they are flawed to your advantage. When I just got out of college, I wanted to join my cousin in his business, which was buying and selling farm produce, namely cocoa and coffee. He and his associate told me upfront, "we know you are a pastor and always talk about holiness, in this business there is a lot of fraud involved. We do not think you will be able to do this trade." Yet, there are people amassing millions by cheating poor and desperate farmers. Such is what we call the prosperity of the wicked, for it is gotten through wickedness.

Choose a side

> **"The LORD detests dishonest scales, but accurate weights find favor with him" (Proverbs 11:1).**
>
> **"Differing weights and differing measures, the Lord detests them both" (Proverbs 20:10).**
>
> **"Dot not use dishonest standards when measuring length, weight, or quantity. Use honest scales and honest weights, an honest ephah and an honest hin. I am the LORD your God" (Leviticus 19:35-36).**

Choose whether you will conduct your affairs in such a way that it will be detestable to the Lord or pleasing to Him. Using what God detests makes you become detestable to Him. That is why in the passage from Deuteronomy 25 previously quoted the Lord says He detests those who deal dishonestly. When your business becomes detestable to God, and eventually yourself, there is no way you can prosper in the true terms of the word. It is only a matter of time for those riches to fly away.

On the other hand, when you deal honesty and accurately, your business finds favor with God. A business that has found favor with God is bound to increase and expand. True prosperity comes from divine favor.

Pay your workers what they deserve
> **"One who oppresses the poor to increase his wealth and one who gives gifts to the rich-both come to poverty" (Proverbs 22:16).**

One way people oppress the poor to increase their wealth is through labor exploitation. They either pay far less what is due these workers who bring in most of the profit or they do not pay at all. This is extreme wickedness, for someone to spend his or her time and effort to serve you and yet you fail to pay them what is due them. If you want true prosperity for your business, make sure to pay the people who work for you what is their due. You can also go an extra mile and pay them more generously within reasonable business profit margins and see how your business grows beyond expectations.

You can start all over

Maybe you recognize that your business dealings have been shady, and have not stood God´s standards. Maybe you hastened to become rich and crashed along the way, because poverty was waiting for you due to dishonest business dealings. You can abandon the shady path and make things right and start over. Here is a promise for you: "**if you are pure and upright, even now he will rouse himself on your behalf and restore you to your prosperous**

state. Your beginnings will seem humble, so prosperous will your future be" (Job 8:6-7).

God wants to rouse Himself on your behalf and make your life and business truly prosperous. It does not matter how little you start, when God rouses Himself on your behalf, the end will be prosperous. You can start all over.

Slow and steady is better

Determine that you would rather be slow and steady than be fast and undulating when it comes to the journey towards prosperity. The temptation to be like every Tom, Dick and Harry who appears to have made it or to be making it may present itself frequently, but the determination to do things God's way is what would keep you from going down that slippery road.

Several years ago, when I was the Branch manager of a microfinance bank, at least four of my colleagues from other branches ended up in jail for diverse manner of fraud. They wanted to get rich fast. I had to lock up one daily cash collector because he was involved in fraud. Another senior colleague in my branch was caught red handed by me, the only thing that kept him from jail was the intervention of the church leaders. One young manager with great promise ended up in jail because he wanted to get rich fast. All these guys destroyed their careers because of an evil eye. They saw loopholes in the system and decided to exploit not, knowing they would one day be caught.

Think of all the scandals that have plagued the financial and banking sectors the world over. People developed all kinds of Ponzi schemes to defraud others because of the quest to get rich fast. Remember, **"Wealth *gained by* dishonesty will be diminished, but he who gathers by labor will increase" (Proverbs 13:11).** This leads us to our next principle, diligence.

Principle #3

Diligence

In the introduction, we said that poverty is sometimes a result or an effect of laziness. In this regard, there is no other cure to poverty than to work hard. This is one of the virtues on which the Bible emphasizes a great deal of importance on.

Show me any individual who became wealthy, not by inheritance, and you have shown me someone who mastered the art of hard work. It is written that, **"Lazy hands make for poverty, but diligent hands bring wealth" (Proverbs 10:4).** Diligence is not mere brut exertion of oneself to achieve a goal, that is, it is not plain hard work. There are several characteristics that qualify diligence and makes it different from brut exertion as we shall see later. But, first, let us discuss what true prosperity is all about.

Two kinds of work

There are two kinds of work; there is work to fulfil destiny and accomplish God's plan for one's life, and there is work to earn a living. Sometimes the two will coincide with one another, however for most people these two have nothing to do with each other. That is, there are many people who are working to earn a living rather than fulfil destiny. What they are doing is not what God created them for, but because they make a living out of it, they have turned to settle therein.

I believe for most of us, if not all of us, we were designed to make a living out of our God ordained purpose and calling. Where working to fulfil destiny is different from working to earn a living, the latter was meant to be a tool to help us accomplish the former.

Let us bring out some differences between the two kinds of work, when what we are doing is for the sole purpose of earning a living. And when we are working to fulfill destiny:

Working to fulfil destiny	Working to make a living
It is God-centered and others-centered John 5:17-19	It is self-centered or family-centered
It flows out of faith and love, 1Thessalonians 1:3	It flows out of earnings
Rewarded by inner satisfaction John 4:31-34	Rewarded by outward gain
Rewards are eternal John 6:27, Ecclesiastes 2:17-23	Rewards are temporal
Needs divine resources Colossians 1:29, 1Peter 4:10-11	Human resources are sufficient

How to develop diligence

Every human being has the tendency to become lazy. It is as if our normal state is to drift towards laziness, unless we consciously make an effort to move in the opposite direction. In this section, let me share with you some keys to develop diligence.

"Therefore, my beloved brethren, be ye steadfast, unmovable, always abounding in the work of the Lord, forasmuch as ye know that your labor is not in vain in the Lord" (1Corinthians 15:58, KJV).

1. Steadfastness:

To be steadfast is to be resolutely or dutifully firm and unwavering. Do not waver from what you believe the Lord has equipped you to do. Be firm in your pursuit of destiny. Resolve it in your own heart that you will not waver.

2. Be unmovable:

In addition to not wavering, be not moved by external happenings. Do not let naysayers and their attitudes cause you to abandon your race

3. Be fully engaged.

Fully give yourself to what you are doing to fulfill destiny. Ecclesiastes 9:10 commands you to do with all your might whatever your hand finds to do.

"**[11] We want each of you to show this same diligence to the very end, so that what you hope for may be fully realized. [12] We do not want you to become lazy, but to imitate those who through faith and patience inherit what has been promised" (Hebrews 6:11-12).**

4. Faith:

While the above passage refers to faith in God, I believe to be diligent, you need to have both faith in God and faith in yourself. Believe that you are capable to being used by God to accomplish the destiny He ordained for you to do. Believe that God is also faithful to reward your hard work.

5. Patience:

Many of us expect instant results. Instant success is a myth that has deceived too many to give up, because results did not come as quick as they thought. There is no body who succeeds instantly. You need to exercise patience in what you are doing to reap the benefits. We shall discuss more on this when we talk about faithfulness and consistence as a key to divine prosperity.

> **"Whatever your hand finds to do, do it with all your might, for in the realm of the dead, where you are going, there is neither working nor planning nor knowledge nor wisdom" (Ecclesiastes 9.10).**

In this verse, the writer lists three characteristics of diligence, namely: planning, knowledge, and wisdom. These lead us to our next points.

6. Planning:

One important aspect of diligence, if not the most important, is the ability to plan. Make specific plans on your business, spiritual, professional, or social projects and set out to execute them. In order to plan well, you need knowledge and wisdom.

7. Knowledge:

For planning to be efficient and effective, you need knowledge, and knowledge is acquired through learning, both formal and informal learning. The verse from Hebrews quoted earlier says to be diligent, you have to imitate others who have succeeded. Diligence requires learning to acquire useful and fruitful knowledge in your domain of business. Many people dive into a business because they see others have succeeded in it, without ever studying or reading about the business, or learning directly from those who have succeeded. With acquired knowledge then comes the application of wisdom.

8. Wisdom:

Wisdom is the right application of knowledge. Sometimes you may need to study more than one business model or ministry model in the direction of your project and discretely choose your own path through your judgments based on the acquired knowledge.

9. Do all as unto the Lord, and in the name of the Lord:

"**[17] And whatever you do, whether in word or deed, do it all in the name of the Lord Jesus, giving thanks to God the Father through him…[23]Whatever you do, work at it with all your heart, as working for the Lord, not for human masters, [24] since you know that you will receive an inheritance from the Lord as a reward. It is the Lord Christ you are serving**" **(Colossians 3:17, 23-24).**

Remember we are talking of divine prosperity. When you want to prosper God´s way, you have to do everything in the name of the Lord and as unto the Lord. When you do things as unto the great God of the universe, you are bound to put in your all, and bring out your best. Or next points comes from the following passage,

"Therefore, since we are surrounded by such a great cloud of witnesses, let us throw off everything that hinders and the sin that so easily entangles. And let us run with perseverance the race marked out for us, [2] fixing our eyes on Jesus, the pioneer and perfecter of faith. For the joy set before him he endured the cross, scorning its shame, and sat down at the right hand of the throne of God" (Hebrews 12:2-3).

10. Get rid of distractions:

Throw away those things that would hinder you in your exercise of diligence. Do not say you will keep them and resist their distractions. The Bible recommends that you throw them away. Be honest with yourself and take stock of those things in your possession, or people in your circle who are just meant to distract and slow down, then be courageous enough to break the links.

11. Tap into the power of expectations:
" for the joy set before Him…"

The joy set before Him were his expectations to rise from the dead and be enthroned at the right hand of God the Father. To fill your heart with expectations, look daily at your goals and plans. Look at what you want to become and uphold it in your heart and mind.

These points on how to acquire diligence apply to both our work to fulfil destiny and our work to make a living, when the two do not coincide. Now, let´s take a look at the rewards of diligence.

The rewards of diligence
1. Dominion:

> "Diligent hands will rule, but laziness ends in forced labor" (Proverbs 12:24).

2. Satisfaction

    > "A sluggard's appetite is never filled, but the desires of the diligent are fully satisfied" (Proverbs 13:4).

3. Wealth ,

    > "All hard work brings a profit, but mere talk leads only to poverty" (Proverbs 14:23).

    > "Lazy hands make for poverty, but diligent hands bring wealth" (Proverbs 10:4).

4. Increase ,

    > "The plans of the diligent lead to profit as surely as haste leads to poverty" (Proverbs 21:5).

Having looked at diligence, in the next key, we will look at another important principle, vital to becoming prosperous, namely, generosity.

Principle #4

Generosity

One important key to true and lasting prosperity is generosity. As human beings, we have the tendency to be generous towards those we love and know, those in our circles of interactions. There is nothing wrong with that, but it is a limitation when we are only open handed towards those who in some way directly or indirectly will repay us. If you ask the average person down the street, they will show you prove of their generosity, albeit you would discover it is limited to those they love or are related with in some way.

Throughout scripture, God's emphasis on generosity has always been towards the poor and needy; those who are not able to repay us in whatever way, directly or indirectly. The Lord Jesus taught that we should give to those who cannot repay us. It is also written that,

"One person gives freely, yet gains even more; another withholds unduly, but comes to poverty. ^{25} A generous person will prosper; whoever refreshes others will be refreshed" (Proverbs 11:24-25).

"He that giveth unto the poor shall not lack: but he that hideth his eyes shall have many a curse" (Proverbs 28:27, KJV).

"The generous will themselves be blessed, for they share their food with the poor" (Proverbs 22:9, KJV).

Be a money lender

God has established a way for you to become rich. It is by lending money to God. The way you lend to God is by giving to the poor. As you give to the poor, you indirectly lend to God, and in due time God will pay you with interest. God can be a debtor to no one. So, when you lend to Him you can be sure that you will regain what you lent to him with interest. Remember, **"He that hath pity upon the poor lendeth unto the Lord; and that which he hath given will he pay him again" (Proverbs 19:17, KJV).**

The Secret

Now ,this is the secret to lasting divine prosperity; whether social, material, financial or spiritual; the secret is giving (see Deuteronomy 15). Give generously to those in need around you, then

i) Your God will bless you in <u>all</u> your work

ii) Your God will bless you in everything you put your hand to.

That is the open door into the blessed kind of life. You see, many people do make gifts, but most often they make gifts to those who do not need the things or who can afford those same things. God says we should be generous towards the poor of the land and not the rich. The corrupt nature of our society has made it such that even the poor will want to offer gifts to the rich. But, listen to what the Word says, **"There will always be poor people in the land. Therefore, I command you to be openhanded toward your brothers and toward the poor and needy in your land" (Deuteronomy 15:11).**

There will always be people whose need you can meet. There will always be people who you are more privileged than, be it financially or materially. Make it a lifestyle to be a blessing to the less privileged around you. There is at least one person you can help. There will always be an opportunity for you to provoke God's blessings through acts of generosity.

Open-handedness is a command and not an option. To be tightfisted is a sin because it is clear-cut disobedience to a command. Your open-handedness must be

i) Towards your brethren

ii) Towards the poor and needy in the land.

That is, God expects you to meet primarily the needs of those in the church (Galatians 6:10), but also that you go beyond the confines of the church to meeting the needs of the unsaved. Your generosity should begin with, but must not be limited to, those in the church. Verse fourteen gives us another startling truth: "Supply him liberally from your flock, your threshing floor and your winepress. Give to him as the LORD your God has blessed you"

Your giving is a proclamation of how far you believe God has blessed you. The degree of your gratitude is reflected in your giving. We can draw the following conclusions about giving:

- Failure to give is a proclamation that God has not blessed you.

- Giving a little is a proclamation that God has blessed you just a little.

- Giving much is a proclamation that God has blessed you much.

- Reducing your giving is a proclamation that God has withdrawn some of His blessings
- Maintaining a certain constant giving is a proclamation that you are not growing in blessing.

Your giving, both to God and to the needy, is either true or false depending on whether it is a true reflection of how God has blessed you or not. To give less than what you ought to is to ask God to reduce your blessing. To give more than you are supposed to is to ask God to increase your blessing and take you to a new level. Your giving is prophetic; your blessing will respond to your giving. Your giving to others and to God will determine your receiving from others and from God.

Now turn with me to the sixteenth chapter of the same book, seventeenth verse;

"Each of you must bring a gift in proportion to the way the LORD your God has blessed you".

You are expected to give in proportion to what God has blessed you. He does not expect you to give in a smaller proportion to what He has blessed you. He does not expect you to give, as a way of life, greater than the proportion to which He has blessed you.

Giving beyond your ability is not the normal but the occasional. Occasionally you can stretch yourself financially, but let it not be the norm, so that those who depend directly on you do not have their basic needs met. You can decide to live in poverty because you want to give to others and to God's work, but your consecration should not be imposed on those for whom you are directly responsible. They are your primary responsibility before anything else. Let us return to our passage in second Corinthians as we move on.

GOD WANTS YOU TO ABOUND
"Remember this: Whoever sows sparingly will also reap sparingly, and whoever sows generously will also reap generously. [7] Each man should give

what he has decided in his heart to give, not reluctantly or under compulsion, for God loves a cheerful giver. [8] And God is able to make all grace abound to you, so that in all things at all times, having all that you need, you will abound in every good work. [9] As it is written:

"He has scattered abroad his gifts to the poor;

his righteousness endures forever."

Now he who supplies seed to the sower and bread for food will also supply and increase your store of seed and will enlarge the harvest of your righteousness. [11] You will be made rich in every way so that you can be generous on every occasion, and through us your generosity will result in thanksgiving to God" (2 Corinthians 9:6-11).

One of the laws which govern life is that you will reap what you sow in the proportion to which you sow, whoever you are and no matter what you sow, all things being equal. Generosity is an avenue for growth in every area of a man's life.

God cannot, and does not, compel you to give (apart from your tithes and offerings which one must) but wants you to decide in your own heart what to give. God's will is that you give out of a heart that overflows. Giving is from the heart and not the head. If you base your giving on calculations, then you will obviously make no progress in your spiritual life.

God's arithmetic does not follow our human logic and so bringing it into your giving will block your blessing. Give, not what you have decided in your head, nor your mind, nor your emotions, but what you have decided in your heart (spirit). For it to bear fruits, the decision must be that of the spirit. When the decision to give springs from your spirit, giving becomes a cheerful exercise and the blessings are reaped. When this happens, you can then expect the following blessings.

i) <u>A revelation of God's ability:</u>

"And God …"

This is the God who created the whole universe. The One who possesses everything there is, visible and invisible. We are talking of the God who brings into existence things which are not and takes out of existence things which are. The One to whom belong all the gold and silver there is, in heaven and on earth. The One who owns the cattle on a thousand hills.

"**And God is** …"

He is not a God of yesterday or of times past. He is a God of today too. He is a God of tomorrow. He spans eternity. He is Jesus Christ the same yesterday, today and forever. He is a God who is up to date. He revealed Himself to Moses as the "I AM that I AM". God wants to be current in your life.

Cheerful giving is just one of those ways which will cause Him to reveal Himself to you in your current situation. How He longs to make Himself real to you. Giving opens the door for him to come in and manifest His ability in you and through you.

"And God is able …"

The extent to which you sow or give generously is the extent to which God will demonstrate His infinite super abilities in your life and through you. When we talk of giving here, we do not limit ourselves to finances. There are a lot more things to give than just money.

You can give your love …

You can give encouragement

You can give hospitality

You can give your wisdom

You can give counsel

… and many more things!

    ii)   <u>Your life will be full of grace</u>.

"And God is able to make all grace abound to you …"

In other words, God wants to fill your life with divine enabling in all that you do. When God's grace is in all you do, yours is a super blessed life. You receive insight that leaves others dumbfounded. You accomplish in one day what others accomplish in a week.

Your whole life will abound with grace!

Grace to remain healthy!

Grace to remain strong!

Grace to make spiritual progress!

Grace to live holy!

Grace to love everybody!

Grace to be at peace with all men!

Grace to live with the most difficult person in the most difficult circumstance!

Grace to receive revelations!

Grace to have a following!

Grace to do all what you have been called to do!

God wants to fill you with the divine ability to function. That is grace! That grace is so that in all things – great things, small things, things in the limelight, things in secret; seemingly insignificant things and things that can be acclaimed; you can excel and be the best. That grace is in all things at all times. All times – in the morning, at noon, in the evening, at night! When you are asleep or when you are awake. Life is a whole lot different for the better when you can tap into God's grace at will.

iii) <u>You will be sufficiently supplied</u>

"Having all you need …"

God wants us to live permanently in a place where all of our needs are met. Material, physical, emotional, moral, mental, financial, social or spiritual needs. Whatever sphere of need, He wants that "having all you need …"

O! There is a place where all our needs can be met. We were not meant to be lopsided. God wants us to be wholly balanced. There are some people who abound financially but are social misfits. Others abound materially and socially, but are retarded as far as the moral and spiritual aspects of life are concerned. God wants you to grow proportionately in all domains so that you will be completely and sufficiently wholesome and balanced.

Many of us are where some of our needs are being met and we rejoice. Some are where most of their needs are being met and they think it is heaven on earth. God wants to take us further, to the place where not just some of our needs, not even most of our needs, but all of our needs are being met.

When the apostle Paul wrote **"And my God will meet all your needs according to His glorious riches in Christ Jesus" (Philippians 4:19)**, he meant just that. He spoke by the Spirit of the Living God. The word of God is true. If you will believe it and act on it you shall reap the fruits of that life of obedient faith.

"Having all you need …". May we all get to that place. There are some who are already there and are enjoying that blessed life. However, it is not a place for a few. There can never be overcrowding there. He has made enough room for each one of us to accommodate those who are in the street called "Having all you need". It is not a place for a privileged few.

iv) <u>"You will be made rich …"</u>

This portrays you as passive. It is God's work in you and for you that makes you rich. That is why the Lord of all glory said" all these things will be added to you". Who is it that does the addition? God of course! You cannot make yourself rich; wholesomely and "balancely" rich, only God can do that. He does that by,

1. <u>Making all grace abound to you</u> (v 8)

    - Grace to make the right choices
    - Grace to make the right decisions
    - Grace to be looked upon with favor
    - Grace to build the right relationships
    - Grace to conceive the right ideas
    - Grace to make the right investments

2. <u>Increasing your store of seed</u> (v 10)

    This is enlarging your capacity to sow in the lives and ministries of others. This is so that you can sow in the kingdom business and thereby reap the fruits thereof. Seed is meant to be sown. The thing is that many of us instead of sowing the increased store of seed God has given us, we convert it to "bread". Seed is for sowing! If you sow the right seeds in the right season, you will sure reap your harvest of a hundred, or sixty, or thirty folds

3. <u>Increasing the harvest of your righteousness</u> (v 10)

This means God will multiply the yield of all that you do for righteousness sake.

4. <u>Giving you the ability</u> (skill, talent, ideas) to make wealth: **"But remember the LORD your God, for it is he who gives you the ability to produce wealth, and so confirms his covenant, which he swore to your forefathers, as it is today" (Deuteronomy 8:18).**

God will make you rich by giving you the ability to make wealth. He will lead you to make the right investments. He will lead you to do the right business in the right seasons.

v) You will be involved in the welfare of others

"… so that you can be generous on every occasion …"

There is a reason, a good, an overriding purpose why God makes you rich. Making you rich is not the end point, but a means to a greater objective God wants to accomplish through you. God wants to make you rich so that He can reach out to the less privileged through you. The phrase "so that" tells you that being made rich is not all about you, but about others.

Now look at the next phrase "you can". This has to do with the power, potential, ability, or capability to do something. It means to be in a disposition, ready to do something. "Can" is to flow freely with some mastery in that which you do. God is making you rich so that you will be in a position ready to help those in need.

Take a look now at the next phrase "Be generous ..." The Father will make you rich so that generosity will become a part and parcel of your life. Generosity must not be foreign to any child of God; it must be built in the very fabric of your being. God does not only want you to practice generosity, but that it becomes like your nature. To be generous means to be kind hearted to freely give to those who are in need. It means to joyfully meet the needs of those you have no obligation towards. God wants you to be generous on every occasion. This means irrespective of the person in need, irrespective of where the need is, when the need arises, or what the need is.

You can become financially rich!

You can become materially rich!

You can become rich in mercy!

You can become rich in love!

You can become rich in service!

You can become rich in encouraging others!

God has shown you the way. It is your responsibility to walk that path.

Principle #5

Faithfulness and consistency

"When Abram was ninety-nine years old, the Lord appeared to him and said, "I am God Almighty; walk before me faithfully and be blameless" (Genesis 17:1).

"Those who work their land will have abundant food, but those who chase fantasies will have their fill of poverty. [20] A faithful person will be richly blessed, but one eager to get rich will not go unpunished" (Proverbs 28:19-20).

These two verses emphasize on the virtues of faithfulness and consistency. The Lord God told Abraham to practice faithfulness in his walk with Him in order to enter the fullness of the blessings that He had in store for him. Many of us do things for the kingdom, but we are not faithful in the execution of our duties. We have ideas deposited in our hearts by the Holy Spirit, but we do not faithfully pursue those ideas, because we are looking for shortcuts to divine prosperity. Some people will rather saw a seed in the false prosperity gospel that invest faithfully in the kingdom or in something that will bring a return in the long run.

One thing that prevents people from faithfulness and consistency is the tendency to chase fantasies. Do not try to catch up with the Joneses in trying to appear to have made it. It is one thing to be rich and another thing to appear rich. You can appear rich and be poor and you can appear poor and be rich. I prefer the later. As it is written,

"There is one who pretends to be rich, yet has nothing at all; *Another* pretends to be poor, yet has great wealth" (Proverbs 13:7, AMP). But, here is the catch, in trying to appear rich: the tendency is to chase fantasies, and fantasies are very expensive in the sense that they deprive you of investing in realities. "Those who work their land…" is a reality. They reap the rewards of rich blessings.

Develop conviction

We are talking here of consistency. The average man has great ideas. What separates people is the consistency with which they pursue their ideas. Consistency flows from conviction. Before you engage in that enterprise, you need to develop deep conviction that, it is what you have to do.

Good returns do not come easily. It takes consistent investments of resources and time. Do not be deceived by overnight sensations. When circumstances stack the odds against your dream, it is your deep convictions that will sustain your endeavors. Many people have broken through on their tenth try. Thomas Edison succeeded with the light bulb after failing a thousand times, literally. But he was convinced of what he wanted to create. That is the source of persistence. Do not throw in the towel so easily.

The Bible says, "**Those who sow with tears will reap with songs of joy. ⁶ Those who go out weeping, carrying seed to sow, will return with songs of joy, carrying sheaves with them" (Psalm 126:5-6).** This means those who brave it against the odds, those who are consistent in their pursuit of their dream will keep at it no matter the difficulties and eventually reap the rewards of their faithfulness. Stop swinging from one idea to the other. Set your head as a flint and pursue one idea at a time until it is established, then begin with the other.

It takes discipline

There is no consistency without resilience, and there is no resilience without discipline. If you want to be resilient and consequently be consistent, you must uphold the virtue of discipline. In writing to his disciple Timothy, towards the end of his second letter, Paul told him, "**Do your best to come to me before winter" (2 Timothy 4:21a).** In this short sentence there are two very important principles of discipline I'll like us to look at:

Do your best

Discipline involves doing the best you can, and using all you have to see something accomplished. To make the difference does not require you to be the best, but it requires you to be at your best no matter how mundane the task may be. The supernatural help and support of God is available to those who are doing their best.

You are not in need of extra support if you are not using all you are supposed to. This entails hard work and commitment to excellence. Your best does not come out until you consciously decide to give it your best efforts. Doing your best will mean sparing nothing that can be used in the process of executing a task, thereby maximizing effectiveness and efficiency.

Set deadlines

Paul told Timothy to do his best to come before winter. That was setting a deadline. If you are to bring change to your life and your world, you will have to set deadlines for yourself. If you do not set deadlines for yourself, it is likely that you will drift into the pit of procrastination. And there are many people trapped in this pit not knowing how to come out of it.

The way to prevent being trapped in this bottomless pit is for you to work with this principle of personal deadlines. It will help you maximize the use of your time and keep you focused. It will also help you do away with distracting activities that steal your attention and enable you pull all your resources towards the execution of your priorities.

When no one believes in you

There is a story of faithfulness, consistency, conviction, and great discipline that I would like us to take a look at. It is the story of Gideon and his men. They had lived in poverty and want for most of their lives. Gideon was disillusioned, fearful, and hiding from his oppressors. Then he had an encounter with divinity (see Judges 6,7,8).

He did not rush to pursue his dream until he had developed deep conviction that, it was what God wanted him to do. He may have spent too long trying to convince himself, but once he got convinced, his conviction became his driving force and source of resilience in the face of great adversity.

He was commissioned by the angel of the Lord, he had dreamed about his triumph, he had received confirmation from the Lord, but he still faced great difficulties that would have cost many to give up, yet he kept the pursuit. It is written,

> **"Gideon and his three hundred men, exhausted yet keeping up the pursuit, came to the Jordan and crossed it. [5] He said to the men of Sukkoth, "Give my troops some bread; they are worn out, and I am still pursuing Zebah and Zalmunna, the kings of Midian."**
>
> **[6] But the officials of Sukkoth said, "Do you already have the hands of Zebah and Zalmunna in your possession? Why should we give bread to your troops?"**
>
> **[7] Then Gideon replied, "Just for that, when the Lord has given Zebah and**

> **Zalmunna into my hand, I will tear your flesh with desert thorns and briers."**
>
> **[8] From there he went up to Peniel and made the same request of them, but they answered as the men of Sukkoth had. [9] So he said to the men of Peniel, "When I return in triumph, I will tear down this tower" (Judges 8:5-9, emphasis mine throughout).**

They were exhausted, yet kept up the pursuit. That is resilience deriving from conviction. However, the people around did not believe in their venture, and refused to support them. They were even mocked by the people they requested help from. But one thing is sure, when no one else believed in them, they believed in themselves and kept on their pursuit.

Do not expect everyone to believe in your dream; you've got to be convinced and believe in yourself, this is what will help you be faithful and consistent. Twice, Gideon made proclamations that could only have arisen out of deep conviction and belief in his God and himself. His consistency and faithfulness brought about a great victory and uplifting out of poverty and want. The end of the story shows a man who became rich by pursuing his God ordained calling.

Principle # 6

Surrendering

I treated the topic of surrendering to the Lord in a very detailed manner in my book "The Blessings of a Surrendered Life: Broken and Blessed". So, I will not repeat the details here. You would do yourself a favor to read it. I will highlight some points which are pertinent to our topic here. Why is surrendering so important? Sometimes God attaches our ability to prosper in things we may not choose to do.

For many people, the Job, business, ministry etc. they are so zealously involved in is not what the Lord wanted them to be doing. When we choose our profession, business, or ministry on the sole basis of our likeability for it, or the potential for financial gain, we bring ourselves under great limitation. Though we may make much gain from such, other vital ingredients to qualify for divine prosperity will be lacking.

Remember the admonishment to **"not despise the day of little beginnings" (Zechariahs 4:10)** because, **"Your beginnings will seem humble, so prosperous will your future be" (Job 8:7).** The path to the prosperous future God has ordained for each one of us usually starts with small beginnings, which many people shun to their own detriment. By surrendering, I mean coming to the place where you are willing to do anything or start anywhere provided it is where God wants you to start.

One of the greatest counsels I have found in the word is in proverbs chapter three verses 5-7a: **"Trust in the LORD with all your heart and do not lean on your own understanding. In all your ways acknowledge Him, and He will make your paths straight. Do not be wise in your own eyes."** (NASB)

What then is dependence on the Lord?

Not leaning on your understanding

Human initiative originates from human understanding of visible things. Often such initiatives lead to actions that are independent of God. Our greatest limitation is leaning on our understanding which can only lead to finite and limited results. The passage above does not say that we should act without understanding, but that we should not act based on our own understanding.

Often, I have realized that my understanding keeps me in the natural and finite realm. But when I put aside my own understanding and depend on the Lord, the results are mind-blowing. We lean on our own understanding because we fail to trust in the Lord with our whole hearts. That is why the verse begins by exhorting us to trust in the Lord with all our hearts. Once this is done, we will cease to depend on our finite understanding and instead submit to the leading of the Holy Spirit.

The Lord wants us to exercise understanding. However, it is not our understanding that He wants us to exercise but His. And He seeks to fill us with the spirit of understanding. Ask the Lord, daily, to fill you with the spirit of understanding. I have prayed this prayer for a while now, and as a result, I increasingly tap from the infinite understanding of the Spirit instead of depending on human finite understanding. We ought to take conscious decisions not to depend on what our minds are able to conceive independent of God.

Acknowledging the Lord in all your ways

What does it mean to acknowledge the Lord? I believe it means to allow Him to take the lead, accept instruction and direction from Him, and acknowledge His infinite knowledge and wisdom. It is giving Him the place He deserves by submitting to His sovereign power and authority. Acknowledging the Lord is refusing to make any move until you know that He is leading the way. He is the One who knows the ending from the beginning and sees every hurdle or obstacle that lies in the way.

In the book of Isaiah, He promised,

> **"I will lead the blind by ways they have not known, along unfamiliar paths I will guide them; I will turn the darkness into light before them and make the rough places smooth. These are the things I will do; I will not forsake them." (Isaiah 42:16).**

The truth is, we often dread the unknown and the unfamiliar paths of life. And it seems that is where the Lord would rather lead us to. And for Him to lead us we have to follow, and to follow will require depending totally on the Lord. It is like you are on a tour in a place you have never been to. You are forced to depend totally on your tour guide.

In many instances we have been forced to rely on human beings for the direction we need because there was no other option. How much more should we depend on the One who knows all things and never fails? To step into the darkness will require dependence on the Lord to shine His light and turn the darkness into light. There are many things we will never accomplish in life until we come to the point where we are totally, wholly, and completely dependent on the Lord.

Again, He says,

> **"Who among you fears the LORD and obeys the word of his servant? Let the one who walks in the dark, who has no light, trust in the name of the LORD and rely on their God. But now, all you who light fires and provide yourselves with flaming torches go, walk in the light of your fires and of the torches you have set ablaze. This is what you shall receive from my hand: You will lie down in torment" (Isaiah 50:10-11).**

Sometimes, even when we are walking in obedience in response to the word of the Lord from the mouth of His servant, we may still find ourselves in total darkness and uncertainty. At that point the enemy takes advantage of many and entangles them in the web of disillusionment. At such a time, you can choose to trust and rely on the Lord, believing His word, or you can choose to light your own fire and eliminate the darkness. The Lord exhorts us to choose the former. If you, however, choose to light your own fire by devising your own schemes, the end result will be torment for your soul.

The Lord has promised to turn the darkness we encounter into light before us. We must exercise patience even when we think the darkness is lasting longer than expected. Acknowledge the Lord by staying put until He shines His light. This is dependence!

May the Lord, by His tender mercies, bring us to the point of total dependence so that we can enjoy its fruits. As part of the benefits of total surrender, our paths will be made straight and the rough places made smooth. Isn't that glorious? It pays to depend on the Lord, and the wise in heart refuse to depend on their own understanding.

Do not be wise in your own eyes

Human wisdom was given us by the Lord, but it cannot, and should never replace divine wisdom in the life of a believer. Wisdom is the right application of knowledge. However, as believers, we are called to operate in a realm where human wisdom only amounts to folly. What we need is the spirit of wisdom, which is the wisdom of the omniscient God.

The Lord wants us to rise to the level of operating in divine wisdom. But we can only get there when we refuse to be wise in our own eyes, refusing to trust even our most appropriate judgment or decision taken independent of Him.

Just take a look at the benefits of surrender outlined in this passage:

> **[13] "Yet if you devote your heart to him and stretch out your hands to him,**
> [14] if you put away the sin that is in your hand and allow no evil to dwell in your tent,
> [15] then, free of fault, you will lift up your face; you will stand firm and without fear.
> [16] You will surely forget your trouble, recalling it only as waters gone by.

> **¹⁷ Life will be brighter than noonday,
>   and darkness will become like morning.
> ¹⁸ You will be secure, because there is hope;
>   you will look about you and take your rest in safety.
> ¹⁹ You will lie down, with no one to make you afraid,
>   and many will court your favor**" (Job 11:13-19, emphasis mine)

People will seek your favor
"…and many will court your favor."

We earlier saw that when we surrender completely to the Lord, He makes our life bright and causes nations and kings to come to the light of our dawn. Besides this, when you surrender to the Lord, instead of rejection, people will begin to court your favor. They will want to identify with you and be associated with you. This is a direct effect of the glory of the Lord that rises upon you as a result of absolute surrender. We have seen people attracted to the sweet-smelling aroma of the anointing. This however, is child's play compared to the attraction that the glory brings.

In addition, as we will see, surrendering to the Lord puts you in a position of authority and divine influence. When this position of divine influence becomes evident to people, they tend to court your favor. This is because, when you are surrendered to God, the aroma of His glory flows in you and from you to those around. This aroma attracts people to the ministry that God is doing through you.

Of Asher, it is written, **"Most blessed of sons is Asher; let him be favored by his brothers, and let him bathe his feet in oil" (Deuteronomy 33:24).** What a blessing! What a position to be in, where everyone shows you favor!

Friends in High Places

When people know that you have friends in high places, they want to associate with you and court your favor, because you become a gateway to high places. The Bible talks of the days when "… **ten people from all languages and nations will take firm hold of one Jew by the hem of his robe and**

say, 'Let us go with you, because we have heard that God is with you'" (Zechariah. 8:23).

Beloved brethren in the Church of the Firstborn, these are the days. But until we surrender and flow in His will so that His glory and favor are evident upon us, we will not experience this. Are you not tired of men hiding from you when they see you with your Bible? Are you not tired of being turned down because you are born again?

We are in the days of His favor upon the Church. It is time for the nations to court our favor. It is time for them to run to us with their needs and troubles. It is time for them to seek us for solutions from above. But we must get to a state of absolute surrender to the will of He who rules over all.

We must surrender our own wisdom so that He fills us with divine wisdom. When His glory rises upon you, those who hid from you will come running after you. Those who mocked will celebrate you.

Job was so blessed that people courted his favor. In his own words he described his life:

> **"People listened to me expectantly, waiting in silence for my counsel. After I had spoken, they spoke no more; my words fell gently on their ears. They waited for me as for showers and drank in my words as the spring rain. When I smiled at them, they scarcely believed it; the light of my face was precious to them" (Job 29:21-24).**

As you surrender to the Lord, may people long to hear you. May they listen to you with expectation! May they seek your counsel! May they long to see you smile at them! May the light of your face be precious to them! Amen!

To surrender is to submit
> **"Submit to God and be at peace with him; in this way prosperity will come to you. Accept instruction from his mouth and lay up his words in your heart. If you return to the Almighty, you will be restored: If you remove wickedness far from your tent and assign your nuggets to the dust, your gold of Ophir to the rocks in the ravines, then the Almighty will be your gold, the choicest silver for you"(Job 22: 21 - - 25).**

Are you looking for prosperity? There is a better way to get prosperous. It is to have prosperity look for you. If all of God's children will submit to God and be at peace with Him always, then prosperity will come looking for them.

To submit oneself would mean to place oneself under or yield to the authority, will, or power of another. It means to surrender wholly and fully to another. That is the way to have prosperity coming to us. In verse 21 that principle will be treated under the key of maturity.

Let's turn to verse 24 and 25, where this principle of surrendering is re-emphasized in a different way. It says giving up one's all, one's possession, is a way of having all of God and what He has. What is that thing you treasure so much? Give it up and God will become your everything. Do you want God to become your gold and choicest silver? Give up everything and surrender totally to God's mighty hand.

Principle #7

A strong relationship with Jesus

King David, in his last days on earth, made a powerful prayer to God, after he had dedicated the wealth he had gotten as king. Part of what he said is, **"Wealth and honor come from you; you are the ruler of all things. In your hands are strength and power to exalt and give strength to all" (1 Chronicles 29:1 2)**.

We said in the introduction that the ability to make wealth comes from God. It seems to me that many people have not understood this, yet. That is why there are many who exchange their souls for false wealth from the devil and his system. If you want to enter into, and enjoy divine prosperity, you need to reach the point where you know, and everything within you agrees, that true wealth and honor comes from the Lord.

There are many people whose relationship with God begin to suffer because of their pursuit of wealth, and end up in the spiritual drain. For these, wealth becomes a curse instead of a blessing.

The need for maturity

Because God is the best father there is in the whole wide universe, there is a degree of prosperity in terms of wealth and riches He would not allow some people to get into, because to them it will be to their detriment.

Growing up, I know of friends who were given more money than they could handle, and it ended up destroying them. The money became a distraction from their studies and a disciplined lifestyle. Because the Lord sees the end from the beginning, He blesses us in such a way so that all our needs are met, but we are not wealthy. This is the minimum for any child of the King, every need met!

But, because life is not just about us, we need to reach out to others and be a blessing to the world around us. Being wealthy makes us fulfill this calling, stress-free.

We become mature sons and daughters when we realize that, the blessings that flow through our hands were meant to be extended to those around us. When we come to the point that the kingdom, its people, and its potential citizens are central to the blessings that the King pours in our lap, we have begun attaining to the maturity of the saints. One characteristic of children is that they hoard and are self-centered.

Spiritual immaturity is the greatest limitation to entering the life of abundance of blessings. The apostle Paul described the condition of most of us in the following words:

> **"What I am saying is that as long as an heir is underage, he is no different from a slave, although he owns the whole estate. ² The heir is subject to guardians and trustees until the time set by his father. ³ So also,**

when we were underage, we were in slavery under the elemental spiritual forces of the world" (Galatians 4:1-3).

The real questions are, "Can God trust you with true wealth?". "Can you be blessed and become a blessing to others and to Kingdom expansion?"

What a strong relationship looks like
" And observe what the LORD your God requires: Walk in his ways, and keep his decrees and commands, his laws and requirements, as written in the Law of Moses, so that you may prosper in all you do and wherever you go" (1 Kings 2: 3).

Walking in the ways of God is a sure path to the place of abundant prosperity. When we allow the Spirit of God in us, and the word of God with us, to determine what we do and how we do it, then we are walking in the ways of God and keeping His commands. As such, prosperity will be ours in whatever we do. In a sense, your prosperity is independent of what you are doing. The Bible says you will prosper in all you do, wherever you are doing it. Your prosperity is tied to your obedience to the word and the voice of God.

David himself had lived and followed the advice he was giving to his son Solomon in the passage cited above. Since he was a man of the word of God, he was drawing his inspiration from an ancient principle given by Moses to Israel as they were about to get into the Promised Land:

> **"Walk in all the way that the LORD your God has commanded you, so that you may live and prosper and prolong your days in the land that you will possess" (Deuteronomy 5: 33) and "Carefully follow the terms of this covenant, so that you may prosper in everything you do" (Deuteronomy 29: 9).**

The power of God's Word:
> **"Do not let this Book of the Law depart from your mouth; meditate on it day and night, so that you may be careful to do everything written in it. Then you will be prosperous and successful" (Joshua 1: 8).**

This principle goes beyond just obeying the word of God, but storing it up in your heart, ruminating on it and proclaiming it in different situations. The word of God is reactive and effective. If we shall learn to speak God's word to any and every circumstance, then we are sure to live prosperous lives. When we meditate on the word of God, we store it up in our hearts and hence we know what to say and when and how.

The Hebrew word translated as "meditate" in our English Bible is "hagah" which could also mean to murmur in pleasure, to mutter, to speak, to talk, or to utter. Thus, we shouldn't just ponder on God's word to ourselves (mutter) we should speak it to situations and declare what it says.

Deciphering Divine instruction
"I will instruct you and teach you in the way you should go; I will counsel you with my loving eye on you" (Psalm 32:8).

A product of spiritual maturity and a strong relationship with Jesus is the ability to decipher divine instruction. Your prosperity is tied to the instruction you decipher and implement. If you speak with Christians who are prosperous, I can guarantee they will tell you, they once did sometime very ridiculous, which they believed was a divine instruction to them. Think of the Shunamite and Elijah, and the prophet´s wife and Elisha.

Remember Isaac, how in the midst of severe famine he received divine instruction to sow in the land of famine instead of moving away as he initially planned. In obedience to divine instruction, he sowed in the land and reaped a hundredfold return. He became very wealthy in the midst of famine, because he rightly decoded divine instruction.

What about Jacob? In the midst of exploitation and suffering at the hands of his uncle Laban, he received divine instruction in a dream that led to him becoming very wealthy. In both cases faith and obedience were central in their relationship with God.

He sometimes speaks through others
"Whoever gives heed to instruction prospers, and blessed is he who trusts in the LORD" (Proverbs 16: 20).

There is no one who knows everything. There are times when our tested and proven principles or ideas would need adjustments which we might not be aware of. An open mind to the ideas and instructions of others is a sure way to be prosperous.

Nothing leads to quick ruin and poverty like sticking to old ways and ideas and methods. The Bible says, **"There is a way that seems right to a man, but at the end it leads to death" (Proverbs 14: 12).** The word "death" is translated in some versions as "destruction". God's ways and laws are eternal and unchanging, but the method He uses varies from individual to individual and from circumstance to circumstance. This is why we must be open to the instructions of others and to the leadership of the Spirit of God, in order to avoid the pitfalls and the roadblocks to the place of abundant prosperity.

How open are you to instruction which may seem contrary to your thought-out plans or methods? How open are you to new ideas and principles? To become, and to remain prosperous, you must follow the principle of openness.

Principle #8

Understand the power of the blessing

The Power of the blessing
"The blessing of the Lord brings wealth, without painful toil for it" (Proverbs 10:22, NIV).

"The blessing of the Lord makes *one* rich, and He adds no sorrow with it" (Proverbs 10:22, NKJV).

What makes one rich in the true sense of the word is the blessing of the Lord. The added advantage is that it adds no sorrow to the wealth it brings. There are many rich people whose life you wouldn´t want in spite of all their riches. Why? Because of the sorrow they are experiencing. That is why many of them have to take drugs to try to abate their pain and sorrow. When they can't bear it anymore, they resort to suicide. It's as if, it is no longer a surprise when the rich commit suicide.

Until you know the true source of a man's wealth, it is folly to admire him or desire his place. It is the blessing of the Lord that makes the difference between people of equal potentials. The one with less potential plus the blessing of the Lord is greater than the one with more potential without the blessing. The blessing tips the scales to incomparable levels. And God has committed men to transmit His blessings to us.

There is power in blessing. Jacob was placed ahead of his older twin Esau by the power of the blessing through Isaac. The blessing of Jacob placed Ephraim ahead of Manasseh. When God initially created man, even before the fall, He commissioned man with a blessing for dominion and increase. When He called Abraham, He promised to bless him, but that blessing was only set in motion by Melchizedek as seen below.

Abraham Understood the power of the blessing

> "'Then Melchizedek king of Salem brought out bread and wine. He was priest of God Most High, [19] and he blessed Abram, saying, "Blessed be Abram by God Most High, Creator of heaven and earth. [20] And praise be to God Most High, who delivered your enemies into your hand. Then Abram gave him a tenth of everything" ' (Genesis 14:18-20).

The blessing is an important aspect of life you cannot neglect. There are fathers and mothers in life God has ordained to speak the blessing into your life. Usually, they are your biological parents. But also, spiritual parents can be conduits of the blessing. That is why Jesus died so that the blessing of Abraham might come to us the Gentiles.

After Abraham received the blessing of Melchizedek, he was so confident that his life was on course for the blessing the Lord had promised him that he refused accepting gifts from the king of Sodom:

> "But Abram said to the king of Sodom, `with raised hand I have sworn an

oath to the Lord, God Most High, Creator of heaven and earth, [23] **that I will accept nothing belonging to you, not even a thread or the strap of a sandal, so that you will never be able to say, 'I made Abram rich' " (Genesis 14:22-23).**

When the blessing is spoken into your life and you grasp the power of it, your focus shifts from men to Jehovah Jireh, who is the source of all true riches. You enter into a realm of rest that the average human knows nothing of. You cease from fighting with men or manipulating the system set up by men. With the shift in focus, comes unexpected open doors for the wealth of the heathen to be transferred into your life.

It worked for Jacob

"May God Almighty bless you and make you fruitful and increase your numbers until you become a community of peoples. [4] *May he give you and your descendants the blessing given to Abraham,* **so that you may take possession of the land where you now reside as a foreigner, the land God gave to Abraham."** [5] **Then Isaac sent Jacob on his way, and he went to Paddan Aram, to Laban son of Bethuel the Aramean, the brother of Rebekah, who was the mother of**

Jacob and Esau" (Genesis 28:3-5, emphasis added).

The blessing given to Abraham was transmitted to Jacob through the words of Isaac. Although all of Abrahams descendants were candidate for the blessing, there was a special dimension only Jacob entered, because of the implementation by Isaac. We cannot overemphasize the role of human vessels as conduits of the divine blessing.

Jacob, who left with his father's house with just a staff, and no physical inheritance from his father Isaac, was more prosperous than his brother who took the physical inheritance but missed the blessing. When the blessing is spoken over your life, you carry it wherever you go and it works wonders for you.

You are a candidate
> **"He redeemed us in order that the blessing given to Abraham might come to the Gentiles through Christ Jesus, so that**

by faith we might receive the promise of the Spirit" (Galatians 3:14).

Through the death of our Lord Jesus Christ on the cross, you and I became candidates for the blessing that was given to Abraham. There are two conduits of that blessing into your life: the blessing of a spiritual father or mother spoken over you, and the declaration of your words in agreement with what the Bible says.

Speaking the word over your life is essential, but might not be a sufficient condition to fully enter into the blessing of Abraham. The blessing that flows through the word you declare over yourself and the blessings of the words of a father or mother work together to bring you into experiencing the blessing of Abraham that has been made yours through the death of the Lord Jesus Christ.

Principle #9

Put God's Kingdom first

In Matthew 6:33, the Lord Jesus Christ made a very satisfying statement on which anyone could stake their life. He said, **"But seek ye first the kingdom of God, and his righteousness; and all these things shall be added unto you"**. The implication is that when we make God´s Kingdom and His righteousness our priority in life, we graduate from a life of lack. It is not just seeking God´s kingdom or His righteousness, it is seeking both.

We learn in the Bible that Christ Jesus has become our righteousness from God. When we become seekers of Jesus Christ and the spreading of His kingdom which happens through the preaching of the authentic Gospel, the Gospel of the cross that saves from sin, we are making Christ and His Kingdom our priority in life. This means at the minimum; we should have all of our needs met. "All these things" mentioned in the above verse were listed in the earlier verses of the same chapter of Matthew.

While many preachers misquote the passage as "all other things", the Lord was speaking about the things He had previously described. This includes what you eat and drink, what you wear (verse 24-31) and by implication where you live and how you move from one place to another.

Therefore, poverty and lack, in all forms, especially of the basic necessities of life, is never God´s will for any of His children. The Lord Jesus said, the Father knows that we need these basics and that when we make His kingdom our primary focus, they become readily available. Let us see a case in the Bible where some people lived in lack of the basics because of neglect of God´s Kingdom.

Working like an elephant, reaping like an ant

> "Then the word of the Lord came through the prophet Haggai: [4] "Is it a time for you yourselves to be living in your paneled houses, while this house remains a ruin?"
>
> [5] Now this is what the Lord Almighty says: "Give careful thought to your ways. [6] You have planted much, but harvested little. You eat, but never have enough. You drink, but never have your fill. You put on clothes, but are not warm. You earn wages, only to put them in a purse with holes in it" (Haggai 1:3-6).

Maybe you can identify with some of these descriptions; your basic needs of food and drink and clothing are not met. You work like an elephant but eat like an ant. It may be, because like them, you are living in neglect for the things of God. You have put your own needs above the needs of His kingdom.

At the time of the return from exile, the Israelites had built houses for themselves and left the temple in ruins. They kept procrastinating building the Temple. They had good intentions to do it, but kept saying to themselves, "the time has not yet come".

It is an afront to God´s sovereignty when we put our needs above those of the Kingdom. When we make our lives about us instead of Him, we challenge Him to act otherwise. I am sure these individuals thought the devil was the cause of their lack and want, but it was God Himself who was the reason of their life of lack and want. They could have spent eternity binding the devil and the spirit of poverty, but nothing would have changed, why? Because God was responsible. Look at what the Lord said to them:

> **"Give careful thought to your ways. [8] Go up into the mountains and bring down timber and build my house, so that I may take pleasure in it and be honored," says the Lord. [9] "You expected much, but see, it turned out to be little. What you brought home, I blew away. Why?" declares the Lord Almighty. "Because of my house, which remains a ruin, while each of you is busy with your own house. [10] Therefore, because of you the heavens have withheld their dew and the earth its crops. [11] I called for a drought on the fields and the mountains, on the grain, the new wine, the olive oil and everything else the ground produces, on people and livestock,**

and on all the labor of your hands" (Haggai 1:7-11, emphasis added).

So, you see that God is the one who blew their income away, not the devil. He was the one who called for a drought on all the labors of their hands, not the devil. Living in neglect for the things of God is an open door to the curse of poverty.

When we invest far more that we reap returns, it might be a sign of operating under this curse of poverty. When our income never seems to satisfy our needs, it's a sign of financial limitation. Some people think that the answer to poverty is to work the more. There is a place for hard work, but hard work doesn't answer everything. Some people take up second and third jobs, but nothing seems to change. This is because, the root cause of neglect of His Kingdom is not addressed.

You may ask, "why do unbelievers prosper?" My response is twofold: first you have not understood what true prosperity is all about. You need to reread the introduction. Second, they do not operate under the rules of the Kingdom, just like you do not operate under the rules of the dominion of satan.

When the people repented and started rebuilding the Temple, the Lord said to them,

> **"Now give careful thought to this from this day on—consider how things were before one stone was laid on another in the Lord's temple. ¹⁶ When anyone came to a heap of twenty measures, there were only ten. When anyone went to a wine vat to draw fifty measures, there were only twenty. ¹⁷ I struck all the work of your hands with blight, mildew and hail, yet you did not return to me,' declares the Lord. ¹⁸ 'From this day on, from this twenty-fourth day of the ninth month, give careful thought to the day when the foundation of the Lord's temple was laid. Give careful thought: ¹⁹ Is there yet any seed left in the barn? Until now, the vine and the fig tree, the pomegranate and the olive tree have not borne fruit.**
>
> **"'From this day on I will bless you'" (Haggai 2:15-19).**

God was asking them to compare their lives before they put His Kingdom first and after they put His Kingdom first, and noticed the great change.

There was increase in their harvest. Their turnaround in attitude also marked a turnaround for the better in their finances.

You can turn things around for yourself too, by beginning to put God´s kingdom first. Look for ways you can promote the Kingdom and do it. You will be surprised at how quickly breakthrough will come.

Principle #10

Sacrifice and Covenant with God

We saw from principle #9, the importance of putting first the Kingdom of God in helping us enter the blessed and prosperous life. Here, let´s briefly talk about the power of sacrifice as a launch path into the realm of prosperity.

Covenant through sacrifice

One way to get into covenant with God is through sacrifice for the cause of the Gospel. The Lord said**, "gather my saints together unto me; those that have made a covenant with me by sacrifice" (Psalm 50:5).** Those who understand and employ the power of sacrifice get into covenant blessing of wealth and abundance. Read through the Bible and show me one covenant person who did not walk in financial sufficiency! On the contrary, those who established covenant through sacrifice walked in abundance.

When the Lord promised Abraham that He was going to make him great and establish a covenant with, and multiply his descendants (Genesis 15:4-7), Abraham asked a very important question, **"Sovereign Lord, how can I know that I will gain possession of it?" (Genesis 15:8),** and this was the response from divinity**, "⁹ So the Lord said to him, "Bring me a heifer, a goat and a ram, each three years old, along with a dove and a young pigeon" (Genesis 15:9).**

When Abraham asked how he could be sure this promise will be accomplished, the Lord asked him to bring a sacrifice. The sacrifice was to establish a covenant of blessing and guarantee the fulfillment of the promise. We can go on to David and Solomon and many others.

You too, can break the cycle of poverty through sacrifice to kingdom purposes. However, because of the deceitful men out there, do not let anybody coax you into it, let it flow from your personal dealings with God, and you will be surprised at the results.

Covenant of Tithes and offerings

Another area of financial covenant with God is the area of tithes and offering. When God called Abraham, He promised to bless him and make him great. That blessing was implemented when Abraham met Melchizedek and offered him a tenth of the spoils. In Genesis 12, the Lord said to Abraham,

> **"I will make you into a great nation,
>   and I will bless you;
> I will make your name great,
>   and you will be a blessing.
> [3] I will bless those who bless you,
>   and whoever curses you I will curse;
> and all peoples on earth
>   will be blessed through you" (Genesis 12:1-3)**

The promise to be blessed was now implemented by the priest of the MOST High God:

"Then Melchizedek king of Salem brought out bread and wine. He was priest of God Most High, [19] and he blessed Abram, saying, 'Blessed be Abram by God Most High, Creator of heaven and earth. [20] And praise be to God Most High, who delivered your enemies into your hand.' Then Abram gave him a tenth of everything" (Genesis 14:18-20, emphasis mine).

The tenth was to seal the blessing and establish a covenant of financial prosperity, that is why Abraham turned down the offer from the king of Sodom. Because he understood that he was in a financial covenant with God through the promise, the actual blessing, and the sealing of the blessing. So, before the law there was tithing, during the law there was tithing, and after the law there is tithing.

God's challenge to you

There is only one invitation from the Lord, as recorded in the Word, to test Him. It is in the domain of tithing. You need to understand that every child of God pays tithe. You either pay it to the devourer or to God. Those who refuse to pay tithes fail to enter into the blessings that are attached to tithing, but in addition, they open the door into their finances to the devourer.

I am yet to see a faithful tither who lives in poverty. The Lord says when you are faithful with your tithes, He will open the windows of heaven and poor so much blessing into your life that you will be forced to share with others, because you won´t have enough room to contain it for yourself.

Another thing is that when you fail to pay your tithes, you are robbing God. And no one who robs God can walk under the divine blessing. This is what is written,

> [8] "Will a mere mortal rob God? Yet you rob me.
>
> "But you ask, 'How are we robbing you?'
>
> "In tithes and offerings. [9] You are under a curse—your whole nation—because you are robbing me. [10] Bring the whole tithe into the storehouse, that there may be food in my house. Test me in this," says the Lord Almighty, "and see if I will not throw open the floodgates of heaven and pour out so much blessing that there will

not be room enough to store it. ¹¹ I will prevent pests from devouring your crops, and the vines in your fields will not drop their fruit before it is ripe," says the Lord Almighty. ¹² "Then all the nations will call you blessed, for yours will be a delightful land," says the Lord Almighty (Malachi 3:8-12).

As a young believer, this verse was shared with me by the person who was counselling me. Within a month when I received my student allowance, I immediately gave eleven percent to the Lord. After a few months I increase it to twelve, then to fifteen percent, then to twenty percent.

By the time I was four years old in the Lord I was giving thirty percent of my income to the Lord. I had found a source of blessing and increase. In fact, my spiritual mother had to call me and ask me to go back at twelve or fifteen percent and increase gradually.

When I look back, I do not regret giving to God sacrificially. It opened doors for me to be blessed financially. For seven years, I studied in the USA, two and a half years for a Masters degree as a certified Physics teacher. I paid my fees and tuition just for the first semester and had financial assistance from a Christian organization for the other four.

As a doctoral student in the University of Maryland, College Park, I had a graduate teaching assistantship for nine semesters. These fees, tuition, and living expenses could amount to hundreds of thousands of dollars, which I could never have been able to afford. While others graduated with huge student loan debts, I was debt free upon graduation. You see, God is faithful to His word and principles outlined therein. You can only neglect them to your disadvantage, and consistently respect them to your blessing and increase.

In Conclusion

God wants us to prosper, to make reasonable progress in the journey of life. As you look back at your yesterday, you should see your today much better in terms of becoming the man, woman, boy or girl your creator designed you to become. Remember that the ultimate goal of wealth is to be liberated to function in the office of an Ambassador of Christ. Wealth makes it possible to do all that which you are called to do.

Many people feel limited by lack of finances when it comes to accomplishing their God ordained purpose. God's plan is for His people to become employers. When you become an employer, it frees up your time to function in the capacity of an ambassador of the cross of Jesus and gives you a greater sphere of influence to harness both human and material resources for the expansion of the Kingdom of Christ on earth.

This is a promise of His:

> **"Strangers will shepherd your flocks;**
> **foreigners will work your fields and vineyards.**
> **⁶ And you will be called priests of the Lord,**
> **you will be named ministers of our God.**
> **You will feed on the wealth of nations,**
> **and in their riches you will boast" (Isaiah 61:5-6).**

When strangers feed your flock and foreigners work your fields, it means you become an employer. Others are working for you. The purpose of this is so that you will be called priests of the Lord and ministers of your God.

One way to fulfil ministry is to become an employer. Start that company, business, school, clinic etc. and watch God causes it expand beyond your wildest dreams. You feed on the wealth of the nations and boast in their riches because they have become yours. The easiest way to transfer wealth from others to yourself is to create a company that meets the needs of people around you.

www.ingramcontent.com/pod-product-compliance
Lightning Source LLC
Chambersburg PA
CBHW030155100526
44592CB00009B/291